To

Sue Valentine

From

Sr. Phil (DSOP)

Date

Aug 1, 2017

Ellie Claire™ Gift & Paper Expressions
Brentwood, TN 37027
EllieClaire.com

Whispers of Grace: Celebrating the Hope of New Life
© 2013 by Ellie Claire, an imprint of Worthy Media, Inc.

ISBN 978-1-60936-868-5

Scripture quotations are taken from the following sources: The Holy Bible, King James Version (kjv). The Holy Bible, New International Version®, niv®. Copyright © 1973, 1978, 1984, 2011 by Biblica, Inc.® All rights reserved worldwide. The Holy Bible, New King James Version (nkjv). Copyright © 1982 by Thomas Nelson, Inc. The New American Standard Bible® (nasb), copyright © 1960, 1962, 1963, 1968, 1971, 1972, 1973, 1975, 1977, 1995 by The Lockman Foundation. The Holy Bible, New Living Translation (nlt), copyright 1996, 2004, 2007 by Tyndale House Foundation. Used by permission of Tyndale House Publishers, Inc., Carol Stream, Illinois 60188. *The Message* (msg). Copyright © 1993, 1994, 1995, 1996, 2000, 2001, 2002. Used by permission of NavPress Publishing Group. The New Century Version® (ncv). Copyright © 2005 by Thomas Nelson, Inc. Good News Translation® (Today's English Version, Second Edition). Copyright © 1992 American Bible Society. Used by permission. All rights reserved.

Excluding Scripture verses and deity pronouns, in some quotations references to men and masculine pronouns have been replaced with gender-neutral or feminine references. Additionally, in some quotations we have carefully updated verb forms and wording that may distract modern readers.

Stock or custom editions of Ellie Claire titles may be purchased in bulk for educational, business, ministry, fundraising, or sales promotional use. For information, please e-mail info@ EllieClaire.com

Compiled by Jill Jones.
Cover and interior design by Gearbox Studio | www.gearboxstudios.com.

Printed in China

2 3 4 5 6 7 8 9 – 18 17 16 15 14

Whispers of Grace

Celebrating the Hope of New Life

Pi Pocket
INSPIRATIONS

Ellie
Claire
gift & paper expressions

...inspired by life
EllieClaire.com

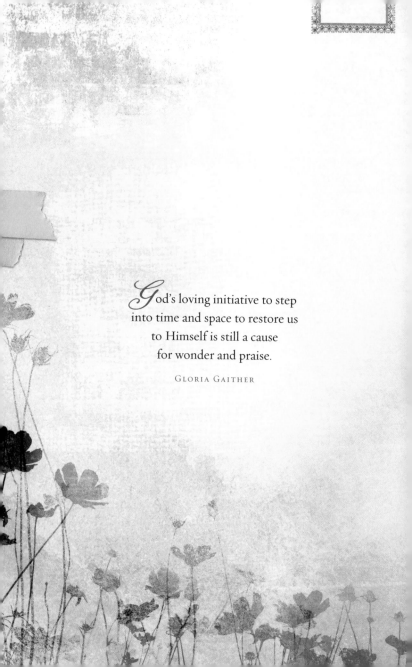

*G*od's loving initiative to step
into time and space to restore us
to Himself is still a cause
for wonder and praise.

GLORIA GAITHER

Contents

The Tune of Grace 6
Grace and Gratitude 8
Infinite Love 10
God's Favor 12
God So Loved 14
Open Hearts 16
The Love of God 18
Perfect Grace 20
God Is Good 22
Loving Father 24
Blessing Upon Blessing 26
Grace Abounds 28
Blessed Assurance 30
No Need to Fear 32
Countless Beauties 34
He Cannot Forget Us 36
Dare to Believe 38
Drawn by Grace 40
The Goal of Grace 42
Redeemed 44
Shining Promises 46
Strong Refuge 48
God Is for Us 50
At Rest in His Grace 52
Every Need 54
Surpassing Grace 56
Grace Is Enough 58
Unshakable Promises 60
River of Delights 62
Personal Grace 64
Promises Fulfilled 66

The Source 68
New Light 70
Eternal Love 72
Joy and Peace 74
Comfort Sweet 76
God of Promise 78
Absolute Certainty 80
Radiant Grace 82
God of Grace 84
Forever Grace 86
Seeking Hearts 88
Immeasurable Love 90
Seek the Lord 92
His Great Love 94
Heart of the Matter 96
Made Whole 98
He Understands 100
Rich Grace 102
He Is More 104
You're Invited 106
Encountering God 108
Full Restoration 110
New Life 112
Our Destiny 114
He Walks with Us 116
He Pays Attention 118
A Message for Us 120
Changed by Grace 122
Sweet Peace 124
Passionate Love 126

The Tune of Grace

Grace comes free of charge to people who do not deserve
it and I am one of those people.... Now I am trying in my
own small way to pipe the tune of grace. I do so because
I know, more surely than I know anything, that any
pang of healing or forgiveness or goodness I have
ever felt comes solely from the grace of God.

PHILIP YANCEY

God loved us, and through his grace he gave us
a good hope and encouragement.

2 THESSALONIANS 2:16 NCV

The secret of life is that all we have
and are is a gift of grace to be shared.

LLOYD JOHN OGILVIE

May the grace of the Lord Jesus Christ, and the love of
God, and the fellowship of the Holy Spirit be with you all.

2 CORINTHIANS 13:14 NIV

Grace is...a boundless offering of God's self to us,
suffering with us, overflowing with tenderness.
Grace is God's passion.

GERALD G. MAY

By Jesus' gracious, kindly Spirit, He moves in our lives,
sharing His very own life with us.... He introduces
the exotic fruits of His own person into the prepared
soil of our hearts; there they take root and flourish.

W. PHILIP KELLER

Receive and experience the amazing grace of...Christ,
deep, deep within yourselves.

PHILIPPIANS 4:23 MSG

Grace and Gratitude

Grace and gratitude belong together like heaven and earth. Grace evokes gratitude like the voice of an echo. Gratitude follows grace as thunder follows lightning.

KARL BARTH

Life itself, every bit of health that we enjoy, every hour of liberty and free enjoyment, the ability to see, to hear, to speak, to think, and to imagine—all this comes from the hand of God. We show our gratitude by giving back to Him a part of that which He has given to us.

BILLY GRAHAM

To be grateful is to recognize the love of God in everything He has given us—and He has given us everything. Every breath we draw is a gift of His love, every moment of existence is a gift of grace, for it brings with it immense graces from Him.

THOMAS MERTON

May you be filled with joy, always thanking the Father. He has enabled you to share in the inheritance that belongs to his people, who live in the light.

COLOSSIANS 1:11–12 NLT

Gratitude consists in a watchful, minute attention to the particulars of our state, and to the multitude of God's gifts, taken one by one. It fills us with a consciousness that God loves and cares for us, even to the least event and smallest need of life.

HENRY EDWARD MANNING

I will bless the LORD at all times;
His praise shall continually be in my mouth.

PSALM 34:1 NASB

Infinite Love

An infinite God can give all of Himself to each of His
children. He does not distribute Himself that each may
have a part, but to each one He gives all of Himself
as fully as if there were no others.... His love has not
changed. It hasn't cooled off, and it needs no increase
because He has already loved us with infinite love
and there is no way that infinitude can be increased....
He is the same yesterday, today, and forever!

A. W. TOZER

～⁂～

Our ever growing soul and its capacities
can be satisfied only in the infinite God.

SADHU SUNDAR SINGH

～⁂～

Give all your worries and cares to God,
for he cares about you.

1 PETER 5:7 NLT

Infinite and yet personal, personal and yet infinite, God
may be trusted because He is the True One. He is true,
He acts truly, and He speaks truly.... God's truthfulness is
therefore foundational for His trustworthiness.

OS GUINNESS

At the very heart and foundation of all God's dealings
with us, however dark and mysterious they may be, we
must dare to believe in and assert the infinite, unmerited,
and unchanging love of God.

L. B. COWMAN

You, being rooted and grounded in love, may be able to...
know the love of Christ which surpasses knowledge.

EPHESIANS 3:17–19 NASB

God's Favor

God longs to give favor—that is, spiritual strength and
health—to those who seek Him, and Him alone. He
grants spiritual favors and victories, not because the one
who seeks Him is holier than anyone else, but in order
to make His holy beauty and His great redeeming power
known.... For it is through the living witness of others that
we are drawn to God at all. It is because of His creatures,
and His work in them, that we come to praise Him.

TERESA OF AVILA

It is not what we do that matters,
but what a sovereign God chooses to do through us.
God doesn't want our success; He wants us.

CHARLES COLSON

Draw near to God and He will draw near to you.

JAMES 4:8 NASB

Each one of us is God's special work of art.
Through us, He teaches and inspires,
delights and encourages, informs and uplifts
all those who view our lives. God, the master
artist, is most concerned about expressing Himself—
His thoughts and His intentions—through what He paints
in our character.... [He] wants to paint a beautiful
portrait of His Son in and through your life.
A painting like no other in all of time.

JONI EARECKSON TADA

God had special plans for me and set me apart for his work....
He called me through his grace.

GALATIANS 1:15 NCV

God So Loved

Who shall separate us from the love of Christ?
Shall trouble or hardship or persecution or famine or
nakedness or danger or sword?... No, in all these things
we are more than conquerors through him who loved us.
For I am convinced that neither death nor life, neither
angels nor demons, neither the present nor the future,
nor any powers, neither height nor depth, nor anything
else in all creation, will be able to separate us from
the love of God that is in Christ Jesus our Lord.

ROMANS 8:35, 37–39 NIV

All the things in this world are gifts and signs of God's
love to us. The whole world is a love letter from God.

PETER KREEFT

The grace of God means something like: Here is your life.
You might never have been, but you are because the party
wouldn't have been complete without you. Here is the
world. Beautiful and terrible things will happen. Don't be
afraid. I am with you. Nothing can ever separate us.
It's for you I created the universe. I love you.

FREDERICK BUECHNER

Nothing can separate you from His love, absolutely
nothing.... God is enough for time, and God is enough
for eternity. God is enough!

HANNAH WHITALL SMITH

For God so loved the world that he gave
his one and only Son.

JOHN 3:16 NIV

Open Hearts

The "air" which our souls need also envelops all of us at
all times and on all sides. God is round about us in Christ
on every hand, with many-sided and all-sufficient grace.
All we need to do is to open our hearts.

OLE HALLESBY

❧

God wants you to know Him as personally as He knows
you. He craves a genuine relationship with you.... He
didn't make us robots, pre-programmed to love Him and
follow Him. He gave us free will and leaves it to us to
choose to spend time with Him. That way it's genuine.
That way it's a real relationship.

TOM RICHARDS

❧

All those who live with any degree of serenity
live by some assurance of grace.

REINHOLD NIEBUHR

What was invisible we behold,
What was unknown is known.
Open our eyes to the light of grace,
Unloose our hearts from fear,
Be with us in the strength of love,
Lead us in the hope of courage.

EVELYN FRANCIS CAPEL

❧

Lord, give me an open heart to find You everywhere,
to glimpse the heaven enfolded in a bud,
and to experience eternity in the smallest act of love.

MOTHER TERESA

❧

God loves you, and we know he has chosen you.

1 THESSALONIANS 1:4 NCV

The Love of God

Our love to God arises out of our emptiness;
God's love to us out of His fullness.

HANNAH MORE

∼❧∼

We are of such value to God that He came to
live among us...and to guide us home. He will go
to any length to seek us, even to being lifted high
upon the cross to draw us back to Himself.

CATHERINE OF SIENNA

∼❧∼

Return to the LORD your God, for he is gracious
and compassionate, slow to anger and abounding in love,
and he relents from sending calamity.

JOEL 2:13 NIV

We have a Father in heaven who is almighty,
who loves His children as He loves His only-begotten
Son, and whose very joy and delight it is to [comfort]
and help them at all times and under all circumstances.

GEORGE MUELLER

A quiet morning with a loving God puts the events
of the upcoming day into proper perspective.

JANETTE OKE

I know that He who is far outside the whole creation
Takes me within Himself and hides me in His arms....
He is my heart, He is in heaven: Both there and here
He shows Himself to me with equal glory.

SYMEON

Perfect Grace

We don't have to be perfect.... We are asked only
to be real, trusting in His perfection to cover our
imperfection, knowing that one day we will finally
be all that Christ saved us for and wants us to be.

GIGI GRAHAM TCHIVIDJIAN

When the time of perfection comes, these partial things
will become useless.... Now we see things imperfectly,
but then we will see everything with perfect clarity.
All that I know now is partial and incomplete,
but then I will know everything completely,
just as God now knows me completely.

1 CORINTHIANS 13:10, 12 NLT

There is no one so far lost that Jesus
cannot find him and cannot save him.

ANDREW MURRAY

Thank You, Jesus, for Your unlimited grace that saves me
from my sins. I receive Your gift of grace. Transform my
life so that I may bring glory and honor to You alone.

MARILYN JANSEN

God is looking for people who will come in simple
dependence upon His grace, and rest in simple faith upon
His greatness. At this very moment, He's looking at you.

JACK HAYFORD

I am not what I ought to be,
I am not what I wish to be,
I am not what I hope to be;
but, by the grace of God,
I am not what I was.

JOHN NEWTON

God Is Good

All we are and all we have is by the...love of God!
The goodness of God is infinitely more wonderful
than we will ever be able to comprehend.

A. W. TOZER

✧

Taste and see that the LORD is good;
blessed is the one who takes refuge in him.
Fear the LORD, you his holy people,
for those who fear him lack nothing.

PSALM 34:8–9 NIV

✧

The Lord's goodness surrounds us at every moment.
I walk through it almost with difficulty,
as through thick grass and flowers.

R. W. BARBER

✧

His compassions never fail.
They are new every morning; great is your faithfulness.

LAMENTATIONS 3:22–23 NIV

All that is good, all that is true, all that is beautiful...be it
great or small, be it perfect or fragmentary,
natural as well as supernatural,
moral as well as material, comes from God.

JOHN HENRY NEWMAN

We walk without fear, full of hope and courage
and strength to do His will, waiting for the endless
good which He is always giving as fast
as He can get us able to take it in.

GEORGE MACDONALD

I will remain confident of this:
I will see the goodness of the
LORD in the land of the living.

PSALM 27:13 NIV

Loving Father

Incredible as it may seem, God wants our companionship.
He wants to have us close to Him. He wants to be
a father to us, to shield us, to protect us, to counsel us,
and to guide us in our way through life.

BILLY GRAHAM

His Spirit joins with our spirit to affirm
that we are God's children.

ROMANS 8:16 NLT

Don't we all long for a father...who cares for us in spite
of our failures? We do have that type of a father. A father
who is at His best when we are at our worst...whose grace
is strongest when our devotion is weakest.

MAX LUCADO

This is your Father you are dealing with, and he knows
better than you what you need. With a God like this
loving you, you can pray very simply.

Matthew 6:7 msg

Nothing we can do will make the Father love us less;
nothing we do can make Him love us more.
He loves us unconditionally with an everlasting love.
All He asks of us is that we respond to Him with
the free will that He has given to us.

Nancie Carmichael

Christ knew His Father and offered Himself unreservedly
into His hands. If we let ourselves be lost for His sake,
trusting the same God as Lord of all, we shall find safety
where Christ found His, in the arms of the Father.

Elisabeth Elliot

Blessing upon Blessing

God is a rich and bountiful Father, and He does not
forget His children, nor withhold from them anything
which it would be to their advantage to receive.

J. K. MACLEAN

~⦿~

Strength, rest, guidance, grace, help, sympathy, love—
all from God to us! What a list of blessings!

EVELYN STENBOCK

~⦿~

You're blessed when you're content with just
who you are—no more, no less. That's the moment
you find yourselves proud owners
of everything that can't be bought.

MATTHEW 5:5 MSG

~⦿~

Lift up your eyes. Your heavenly Father waits
to bless you—in inconceivable ways to make your life
what you never dreamed it could be.

ANNE ORTLUND

If anyone would tell you the shortest, surest way
to happiness and all perfection, he must tell you to make
it a rule to yourself to thank and praise God
for everything that happens to you. For it is certain
that whatever...happens to you, if you thank and praise
God for it, you turn it into a blessing.

WILLIAM LAW

God, who is love—who is, if I may say it this way,
made out of love—simply cannot help but shed blessing
on blessing upon us. We do not need to beg,
for He simply cannot help it!

HANNAH WHITALL SMITH

I will send down showers in season;
there will be showers of blessing.

EZEKIEL 34:26 NIV

Grace Abounds

To pray is to change. This is a great grace.
How good of God to provide a path whereby
our lives can be taken over by love and joy
and peace and patience and kindness and goodness
and faithfulness and gentleness and self-control.

RICHARD J. FOSTER

∽⊷⊶

For God is, indeed, a wonderful Father who longs
to pour out His mercy upon us, and whose majesty
is so great that He can transform us from deep within.

TERESA OF AVILA

∽⊷⊶

God is waiting for us to come to Him with our needs....
God's throne room is always open.... Every single believer
in the whole world could walk into the throne room all
at one time, and it would not even be crowded.

CHARLES STANLEY

The wonder of our Lord is that He is so accessible
to us in the common things of our lives: the cup of water...
breaking of the bread...welcoming children into our
arms...fellowship over a meal...giving thanks. A simple
attitude of caring, listening, and lovingly telling the truth.

NANCIE CARMICHAEL

If God is here for us and not elsewhere, then in fact
this place is holy and this moment is sacred.

ISABEL ANDERS

God is able to make all grace abound toward you,
that you, always having all sufficiency in all things,
may have an abundance for every good work.

2 CORINTHIANS 9:8 NKJV

Blessed Assurance

Peace of conscience, liberty of heart, the sweetness
of abandoning ourselves in the hands of God,
the joy of always seeing the light grow in our hearts,
finally, freedom from the fears and insatiable desires
of the times, multiply a hundredfold the happiness
which the true children of God possess
in the midst of their [trials], if they are faithful.

FRANÇOIS FÉNELON

❦

God Incarnate is the end of fear; and the heart
that realizes that He is in the midst, that takes heed
to the assurance of His loving presence,
will be quiet in the midst of alarm.

F. B. MEYER

❦

In peace I will lie down and sleep,
'for you alone, O LORD, will keep me safe.

PSALM 4:8 NLT

Come, Thou long-expected Jesus, born to set Thy people free;
From our fears and sins release us; let us find our rest in Thee.

CHARLES WESLEY

Today I give it all to Jesus: my precious children,
my mate, my hopes, my plans and dreams and schemes,
my fears and failures—all. Peace and contentment
come when the struggle ceases.

GLORIA GAITHER

A living, loving God can and does make
His presence felt, can and does speak to us
in the silence of our hearts, can and does warm
and caress us till we no longer doubt
that He is near, that He is here.

BRENNAN MANNING

No Need to Fear

We sometimes fear to bring our troubles to God, because
they must seem so small to Him who sits on the circle of
the earth. But if they are large enough to...endanger our
welfare, they are large enough to touch His heart of love.

R. A. TORREY

～∞～

In difficulties, I can drink freely of God's power
and experience His touch of refreshment and blessing—
much like an invigorating early spring rain.

ANABEL GILLHAM

～∞～

Even though I walk
through the darkest valley,
I will fear no evil,
for you are with me;
your rod and your staff,
they comfort me.

PSALM 23:4 NIV

Grasp the fact that God is for you—let this certainty
make its impact on you in relation to what you are up
against at this very moment; and you will find in thus
knowing God as your sovereign protector, irrevocably
committed to you in the covenant of grace, both freedom
from fear and new strength for the fight.

J. I. PACKER

~๑๑~

My God will supply all your needs according
to His riches in glory in Christ Jesus.

PHILIPPIANS 4:19 NASB

~๑๑~

Every action of our lives touches a chord
that vibrates in Eternity.

EDWIN HUBBELL CHAPIN

Countless Beauties

Satisfy us in the morning with your unfailing love,
that we may sing for joy and be glad all our days.

PSALM 90:14 NIV

❧

Our Creator would never have made such lovely days,
and given us the deep hearts to enjoy them, above and
beyond all thought, unless we were meant to be immortal.

NATHANIEL HAWTHORNE

❧

All the world is an utterance of the Almighty.
Its countless beauties, its exquisite adaptations,
all speak to you of Him.

PHILLIPS BROOKS

❧

Worship the LORD in the beauty of holiness!

PSALM 96:9 NKJV

Something deep in all of us yearns for God's beauty,
and we can find it no matter where we are.

SUE MONK KIDD

The joyful birds prolong the strain,
their song with every spring renewed;
the air we breathe, and falling rain,
each softly whispers: God is good.

JOHN HAMPDEN GURNEY

Lord...give me the gift of faith to be renewed
and shared with others each day. Teach me to live
this moment only, looking neither to the past with regret,
nor the future with apprehension. Let love be my aim
and my life a prayer.

ROSEANN ALEXANDER-ISHAM

He Cannot Forget Us

There was a time when if [Jesus] could have, He would
have turned His back on the whole mess and gone away.
But He couldn't. He couldn't because He saw you.
He saw you betrayed by those you love.
He saw you with a body which gets sick
and a heart which grows weak.
He saw you in your own garden
of gnarled trees and sleeping friends.
He saw you staring into the pit of your own failures
and the mouth of your own grave.
He saw you in your own garden of Gethsemane
and he didn't want you to be alone.... He would rather
go to hell for you than to heaven without you.

MAX LUCADO

The great thing to remember is that, though our feelings
come and go, His love for us does not.

C. S. LEWIS

[Jesus] played life against death and death against life...
so that by His death He destroyed our death, and to give
us life He spent His own bodily life. With love, then,
He has so drawn us and with His kindness so conquered
our malice that every heart should be won over.

CATHERINE OF SIENNA

Sing for joy, O heavens!
Rejoice, O earth!
Burst into song, O mountains!
For the Lord has comforted his people and will have
compassion on them in their suffering.
Yet Jerusalem says, "The Lord has deserted us;
the Lord has forgotten us."
I will not forget you! See, I have engraved
you on the palms of my hands.

ISAIAH 49:13–16 NIV

Dare to Believe

Regardless of whether we feel strong or weak in our faith,
we remember that our assurance is not based upon
our ability to conjure up some special feeling.
Rather, it is built upon a confident assurance
in the faithfulness of God. We focus on His
trustworthiness and especially on His steadfast love.

RICHARD J. FOSTER

∼∽

So faith bounds forward to its goal in God,
and love can trust her Lord to lead her there;
upheld by Him my soul is following hard,
till God has fully fulfilled my deepest prayer.

FREDERICK BROOK

∼∽

Trust in the LORD with all your heart;
and lean not on your own understanding.

PROVERBS 3:5 NKJV

Faith is not belief without proof,
but trust without reservations.

ELTON TRUEBLOOD

❧

Trust in your Redeemer's strength...exercise what faith
you have, and by and by He shall rise upon you with
healing beneath His wings. Go from faith to faith
and you shall receive blessing upon blessing.

CHARLES H. SPURGEON

❧

The grace is God's; the faith is ours. God gave us
the free will with which to choose.
God gave us the capacity to believe and trust.

BILLY GRAHAM

❧

I trust in your unfailing love.
I will rejoice because you have rescued me.

PSALM 13:5 NLT

Drawn by Grace

Grace tells us that we are accepted just as we are.
We may not be the kind of people we want to be...
we may have more failures than achievements...we may
not even be happy, but we are nonetheless
accepted by God, held in His hands.

McCullough

Because of our faith, Christ has brought us into
this place of undeserved privilege where we now stand,
and we confidently and joyfully look forward
to sharing God's glory.

Romans 5:2 nlt

He chose us in Him...to the praise of the glory of His
grace, by which He made us accepted in the Beloved.

Ephesians 1:4, 6

There is nothing but God's grace. We walk upon it;
we breathe it; we live and die by it;
it makes the nails and axles of the universe.

ROBERT LOUIS STEVENSON

Grace is something you can never get but can only
be given. There's no way to earn it or deserve it or bring
it about anymore than you can deserve the taste of
raspberries and cream or earn good looks....
A good night's sleep is grace
and so are good dreams.
Most tears are grace.
The smell of rain is grace.
Somebody loving you is grace.

FREDERICK BUECHNER

The Goal of Grace

The goal of grace is to create a love relationship between
God and us who believe, the kind of relationship for
which we were first made. And the bond of fellowship
by which God binds Himself to us is His covenant.

J. I. PACKER

❧

To believe in God starts with a conclusion about Him,
develops into confidence in Him, and then matures
into a conversation with Him.

STUART BRISCOE

❧

I live by faith in the Son of God,
who loved me and gave himself for me.

GALATIANS 2:20 NIV

❧

You have this faith and love because of your hope,
and what you hope for is kept safe for you in heaven.

COLOSSIANS 1:5 NCV

That is God's call to us—simply to be people who are
content to live close to Him and to renew the kind of life
in which the closeness is felt and experienced.

THOMAS MERTON

❧

Not that we deserve it, not that we can earn it,
but that we know how precious and valuable a gift it is.
That's what makes grace so amazing!

❧

Living a life of faith means never knowing where
you are being led. But it does mean loving and knowing
the One who is leading. It is literally a life of faith...a life
of knowing Him who calls us to go.

OSWALD CHAMBERS

Redeemed

Praise the LORD, my soul,
and forget not all his benefits—
who forgives all your sins
and heals all your diseases,
who redeems your life from the pit
and crowns you with love and compassion,
who satisfies your desires with good things
so that your youth is renewed like the eagle's.

PSALM 103:2–5 NIV

When we focus on God, the scene changes.
He's in control of our lives; nothing lies outside
the realm of His redemptive grace. Even when
we make mistakes, fail in relationships, or deliberately
make bad choices, God can redeem us.

PENELOPE J. STOKES

At the cross Christ triumphed over the cosmic powers—
defeating them not with power but with self-giving love.
The cross of Christ may have assured the final outcome,
but battles remain for us to fight.... In all these sufferings,
large and small, there is the assurance of a deeper level of
meaning, of a sharing in Christ's own redemptive victory.

PHILIP YANCEY

I think of my blessed Redeemer,
I think of Him all the day long:
I sing, for I cannot be silent;
His love is the theme of my song.

FANNY CROSBY

The LORD will redeem those who serve him.
No one who takes refuge in him will be condemned.

PSALM 34:22 NLT

Shining Promises

Our feelings do not affect God's facts. They may blow up,
like clouds, and cover the eternal things that we do
most truly believe. We may not see the shining of
the promises—but they still shine! [His strength] is not
for one moment less because of our human weakness.

AMY CARMICHAEL

We do not know how this is true—where would faith
be if we did?—but we do know that all things
that happen are full of shining seed.
Light is sown for us—not darkness.

He knows the way I take; when He has tried me,
I shall come forth as gold.

JOB 23:10 NASB

God's promises are like the stars;
the darker the night the brighter they shine.

DAVID NICHOLAS

I trust You always though I may seem to be lost and in the shadow of death. I will not fear, for You are ever with me. And You will never leave me to face my perils alone.

THOMAS MERTON

❧

God has not promised skies always blue, flower-strewn pathways all our lives through; God has not promised sun without rain, joy without sorrow, peace without pain. But God has promised strength for the day, rest for the labor, light for the way, grace for the trials, help from above, unfailing sympathy, undying love.

ANNIE JOHNSON FLINT

❧

Not one word has failed of all His good promise.

1 KINGS 8:56 NASB

Strong Refuge

We know that [God] gives us every grace, every abundant
grace; and though we are so weak of ourselves, this grace
is able to carry us through every obstacle and difficulty.

ELIZABETH ANN SETON

❧

Why would God promise a refuge unless He knew
we would need a place to hide once in a while?

NEVA COYLE

❧

The LORD is good, a strong refuge when trouble comes.
He is close to those who trust in him.

NAHUM 1:7 NLT

❧

If the Lord be with us, we have no cause of fear. His eye
is upon us, His arm over us, His ear open to our prayer—
His grace sufficient, His promise unchangeable.

JOHN NEWTON

Jesus Christ is no security against storms,
but He is perfect security in storms. He has never
promised you an easy passage, only a safe landing.

L. B. COWMAN

❧

Do not take over much thought for tomorrow. God,
who has led you safely on so far, will lead you on to the
end. Be altogether at rest in the loving holy confidence
which you ought to have in His heavenly Providence.

FRANCIS DE SALES

❧

You are my strong refuge. My mouth is filled with Your
praise and with Your glory all day long.

PSALM 71:7–8 NASB

God Is for Us

Fear not, for I have redeemed you; I have called you
by your name; you are Mine. When you pass through
the waters, I will be with you; and through the rivers,
they shall not overflow you.

When you walk through the fire, you shall not be burned,
nor shall the flame scorch you. For I am the LORD your
God, the Holy One of Israel, your Savior.... Since you
were precious in My sight, you have been honored,
and I have loved you.

ISAIAH 43:1–4 NKJV

It is God to whom and with whom we travel,
and while He is the End of our journey,
He is also at every stopping place.

ELISABETH ELLIOT

Have confidence in God's mercy, for when you think
He is a long way from you, He is often quite near.

THOMAS À KEMPIS

God not only knows us, but He values us highly
in spite of all He knows.... You and I are the creatures
He prizes above the rest of His creation.

Lord Jesus Christ,
I thank You For all the benefits You have won for me,
For all the pains and insults that You have borne for me.
Most merciful redeemer, friend and brother,
May I know You more clearly,
Love You more dearly
And follow You more nearly
Day by day.
Amen.

If God is for us, who can be against us?

ROMANS 8:31 NKJV

At Rest in His Grace

I have sought Thy nearness;
With all my heart have I called Thee,
And going out to meet Thee
I found Thee coming toward me.

YEHUDA HALEVI

Lead me by your truth and teach me,
for you are the God who saves me.
All day long I put my hope in you.

PSALM 25:5 NLT

The God of all grace, who called you to his eternal
glory in Christ, after you have suffered a little while,
will himself restore you and make you strong,
firm and steadfast.

1 PETER 5:10 NIV

There is no rest in the heart of God
until He knows that we are at rest in His grace.

LLOYD JOHN OGILVIE

Guidance is a sovereign act. Not merely does God will
to guide us by showing us His way...whatever mistakes
we may make, we shall come safely home. Slippings and
strayings there will be, no doubt, but the everlasting arms
are beneath us; we shall be caught, rescued, restored.
This is God's promise; this is how good He is. And our
self-distrust, while keeping us humble, must not cloud the
joy with which we lean on our faithful covenant God.

J. I. PACKER

The LORD longs to be gracious to you;
therefore he will rise up to show you compassion.

ISAIAH 30:18 NIV

Every Need

God wants nothing from us except our needs,
and these furnish Him with room to display
His bounty when He supplies them freely.... Not what
I have, but what I do not have, is the first point
of contact between my soul and God.

CHARLES H. SPURGEON

❦

Jesus Christ has brought every need, every joy, every
gratitude, every hope of ours before God. He accompanies
us and brings us into the presence of God.

DIETRICH BONHOEFFER

❦

How calmly may we commit ourselves to the hands
of Him who bears up the world.

JEAN PAUL RICHTER

You can trust God right now to supply all your needs for today. And if your needs are more tomorrow, His supply will be greater also. Knowing God is putting your trust in Him. Trust that He loves you and will provide for your every need. When we know God, we know Him like a personal friend.... God is for us! He will never leave us.

TOM RICHARDS

Each of us may be sure that if God sends us on stony paths He will provide us with strong shoes, and He will not send us out on any journey for which He does not equip us well.

ALEXANDER MACLAREN

You are my strength; I wait for you to rescue me, for you, O God, are my fortress.

PSALM 59:9 NLT

Surpassing Grace

God, being rich in mercy, because of His great love with
which He loved us, even when we were dead in our
transgressions, made us alive together with Christ
(by grace you have been saved), and raised us up with
Him, and seated us with Him in the heavenly places in
Christ Jesus, so that in the ages to come He might show
the surpassing riches of His grace in kindness toward us
in Christ Jesus. For by grace you have been saved through
faith; and that not of yourselves, it is the gift of God; not
as a result of works, so that no one may boast.

EPHESIANS 2:4–9 NASB

❧

God's grace is the oil that fills the lamp of love.

HENRY WARD BEECHER

❧

The LORD is compassionate and gracious,
slow to anger, abounding in love.

PSALM 103:8 NIV

Grace means that God already loves us as much
as an infinite God can possibly love.

PHILIP YANCEY

❧

Before anything else, above all else, beyond everything
else, God loves us. God loves us extravagantly,
ridiculously, without limit or condition.
God is in love with us…God yearns for us.

ROBERTA BONDI

❧

Grace is no stationary thing, it is ever becoming.
It is flowing straight out of God's heart. Grace does
nothing but re-form and convey God. Grace makes
the soul conformable to the will of God. God,
the ground of the soul, and grace go together.

MEISTER ECKHART

Grace Is Enough

Lord...You have given me anything I am or have;
I give it all back to You to stand under Your will alone.
Your love and Your grace are enough for me;
I shall ask for nothing more.

IGNATIUS OF LOYOLA

Soar back through all your own experiences.
Think of how the Lord has led you in the
wilderness and has fed and clothed you every day.
How God has borne with your ill manners,
and put up with all your murmurings
and all your longings after the "sensual pleasures
of Egypt"! Think of how the Lord's grace
has been sufficient for you in all your troubles.

CHARLES H. SPURGEON

My grace is sufficient for you, for My strength
is made perfect in weakness.

2 CORINTHIANS 12:9 NKJV

Let your faith in Christ...be in the quiet confidence
that He will every day and every moment keep you
as the apple of His eye, keep you in perfect peace
and in the sure experience of all the light
and the strength you need in His service.

ANDREW MURRAY

I have come that they may have life,
and that they may have it more abundantly.

JOHN 10:10 NKJV

Unshakable Promises

Commit to hope. There's reason to! For the believer,
hope is divinely assured things that aren't here yet!
Our hope is grounded in unshakable promises.

JACK HAYFORD

❧

God promises to keep us in the palm of [His] hand,
with or without our awareness. God has already made
a space for us, even if we have not made a space for God.

DAVID AND BARBARA SORENSEN

❧

I have told you these things, so that in me
you may have peace. In this world you will have trouble.
But take heart! I have overcome the world.

JOHN 16:33 NIV

❧

Faith allows us to continually delight in life
since we have placed our needs in God's hands.

JANET L. SMITH

Remember you are very special to God as His precious
child. He has promised to complete the good work
He has begun in you. As you continue to grow in Him,
He will teach you to be a blessing to others.

GARY SMALLEY AND JOHN TRENT

Confidence is not based on wishful thinking,
but in knowing that God is in control. There are no
hidden reserves in the promises of God that are meant
to deprive them of their complete fulfillment.

HANNAH WHITALL SMITH

Let us hold tightly without wavering to the hope
we affirm, for God can be trusted to keep his promise.

HEBREWS 10:23 NLT

River of Delights

Your love, LORD, reaches to the heavens, your faithfulness
to the skies. Your righteousness is like the highest
mountains, your justice like the great deep.... How
priceless is your unfailing love, O God! People take
refuge in the shadow of your wings. They feast on the
abundance of your house; you give them drink
from your river of delights. For with you
is the fountain of life; in your light we see light.

PSALM 36:5–9 NIV

God loves us, not because we are lovable
but because He is love, not because He needs to receive
but because He delights to give.

C. S. LEWIS

From God, great and small, rich and poor, draw living
water from a living spring, and those who serve Him
freely and gladly will receive grace answering to grace.

THOMAS À KEMPIS

You alone are the LORD. You made the heavens...the earth
and all that is on it, the seas and all that is in them.
You give life to everything, and the multitudes
of heaven worship you.

NEHEMIAH 9:6 NIV

God's love is like a river springing up in the Divine
Substance and flowing endlessly through His creation,
filling all things with life and goodness and strength.

THOMAS MERTON

Those who drink the water I give will never
be thirsty again. It becomes a fresh, bubbling spring
within them, giving them eternal life

JOHN 4:14 NLT

Personal Grace

All that we have and are is one of the unique
and never-to-be repeated ways God has chosen
to express Himself in space and time. Each of us,
made in His image and likeness, is yet another
promise He has made to the universe that
He will continue to love it and care for it.

BRENNAN MANNING

❧

You have a unique message to deliver, a unique song
to sing, a unique act of love to bestow. This message,
this song, and this act of love have been entrusted
exclusively to the one and only you.

JOHN POWELL

❧

Walk in a manner worthy of the calling with which you
have been called...being diligent to preserve the unity of
the Spirit in the bond of peace.... To each one of us grace
was given according to the measure of Christ's gift.

EPHESIANS 4:1–3, 7 NASB

Priceless in value, we are handcrafted by God,
who has a personal design and plan for each of us.

WENDY MOORE

～⁂～

We have missed the full impact of the Gospel if we have
not discovered what it is to be ourselves, loved by God,
irreplaceable in His sight, unique among our fellow men.

BRUCE LARSON

～⁂～

God's designs regarding you, and His methods of bringing
about these designs, are infinitely wise.

MADAME JEANNE GUYON

～⁂～

We are God's handiwork,
created in Christ Jesus to do good works.

EPHESIANS 2:10 NIV

Promises Fulfilled

The fulfillment of God's promise depends entirely on
trusting God and his way, and then simply embracing him
and what he does. God's promise arrives as pure gift.

ROMANS 4:16 MSG

∽≈∽

Jesus Christ opens wide the doors of the treasure house
of God's promises, and bids us go in and take with
boldness the riches that are ours.

CORRIE TEN BOOM

∽≈∽

God has promised us even more than His own Son.
He's promised us power through the Spirit—
power that will help us do all that He asks of us.

JONI EARECKSON TADA

∽≈∽

We may...depend upon God's promises, for...He will be
as good as His word. He is so kind that He cannot deceive
us, so true that He cannot break His promise.

MATTHEW HENRY

Not one word of all the good words which the LORD
your God spoke concerning you has failed;
all have been fulfilled for you, not one of them has failed.

Christianity is founded on a promise.
Faith involves waiting on a promise. Our hope
is based on a promise. God promised He would
be "with us," not as an unseen ethereal force,
but in the form of a person with a name: Jesus.

MICHAEL CARD

Your promises have been thoroughly tested;
that is why I love them so much.

PSALM 119:140 NLT

The Source

He is the Source. Of everything. Strength for your day.
Wisdom for your task. Comfort for your soul. Grace
for your battle. Provision for each need. Understanding
for each failure. Assistance for every encounter.

JACK HAYFORD

❧

We are forgiven and righteous because of Christ's
sacrifice; therefore we are pleasing to God in spite of our
failures. Christ alone is the source of our forgiveness,
freedom, joy, and purpose.

ROBERT S. MCGEE

❧

The very life of God, epitomized in the love of God,
originates only and always with Him.

W. PHILIP KELLER

❧

For he satisfies the thirsty
and fills the hungry with good things.

PSALM 107:9 NLT

He is the God who made the world and everything in it....
From one man he created all the nations throughout the
whole earth.... His purpose was for the nations to seek
after God and perhaps feel their way toward him and find
him—though he is not far from any one of us.

ACTS 17:24, 26–27 NLT

୭୧

We must drink deeply from the very Source the deep calm
and peace of interior quietude and refreshment of God,
allowing the pure water of divine grace to flow plentifully
and unceasingly from the Source itself.

MOTHER TERESA

୭୧

You are never alone. In your heart of hearts, in the place
where no two people are ever alike, Christ is waiting for
you. And what you never dared hope for springs to life.

BROTHER ROGER OF TAIZÉ

New Light

Into all our lives, in many simple, familiar,
homely ways, God infuses this element of joy
from the surprises of life, which unexpectedly brighten
our days, and fill our eyes with light.

SAMUEL LONGFELLOW

~◦~

God's touch...lights the world with color
and renews our hearts with life.

JANET L. SMITH

~◦~

Each time a rainbow appears, stretching from one end
of the sky to the other, it's God renewing His promise.
Each shade of color, each facet of light displays
the radiant spectrum of God's love—a promise that life
can be new for each one of us.

Brightness of my Father's glory,
Sunshine of my Father's face,
Let thy glory e'er shine on me,
Fill me with Thy grace.

JEAN SOPHIA PIGOTT

It doesn't take a huge spotlight to draw attention
to how great our God is. All it takes is for one committed
person to so let His light shine before men,
that a world lost in darkness welcomes the light.

GARY SMALLEY AND JOHN TRENT

Every good and perfect gift is from above,
coming down from the Father of the heavenly lights.

JAMES 1:17 NIV

Eternal Love

The LORD is like a father to his children, tender and
compassionate to those who fear him. For he knows how
weak we are; he remembers we are only dust.
Our days on earth are like grass; like wildflowers,
we bloom and die. The wind blows, and we are gone—
as though we had never been here. But the love of the
LORD remains forever.... The LORD has made the heavens
his throne; from there he rules over everything.

PSALM 103:13–17, 19 NLT

Amid the ebb and flow of the passing world, our God
remains unmoved, and His throne endures forever.

ROBERT COLEMAN

The reason we can dare to risk loving others is that
"God has for Christ's sake loved us." Think of it!
We are loved eternally, totally, individually, unreservedly!
Nothing can take God's love away.

GLORIA GAITHER

In the morning let our hearts
gaze upon God's love...and in the beauty of that vision,
let us go forth to meet the day.

ROY LESSIN

The impetus of God's love comes from within Himself,
to share with us His life and love. It is a beautiful,
eternal gift, held out to us in the hands of love.
All we have to do is say "Yes!"

JOHN POWELL

He loves us with unfailing love;
the LORD's faithfulness endures forever.

PSALM 117:2 NLT

Joy and Peace

God came to us because God wanted to join us on
the road, to listen to our story, and to help us realize
that we are not walking in circles but moving toward
the house of peace and joy. This is the great mystery...that
continues to give us comfort and consolation: we are not
alone on our journey. The God of love who gave us life
sent us [His] only Son to be with us at all times and in all
places, so that we never have to feel lost in our struggles
but always can trust that God walks with us.

HENRI J. M. NOUWEN

Love comes while we rest against our Father's chest.
Joy comes when we catch the rhythms of His heart.
Peace comes when we live in harmony with those rhythms.

KEN GIRE

God give me joy in the common things:
In the dawn that lures, the eve that sings.
In the new grass sparkling after rain,
In the late wind's wild and weird refrain;
In the springtime's spacious field of gold,
In the precious light by winter doled....
God give me joy in the tasks that press,
In the memories that burn and bless;
In the thought that life has love to spend,
In the faith that God's at journey's end.

THOMAS CURTIS CLARK

May the God of hope fill you with all joy
and peace as you trust in him.

ROMANS 15:13 NIV

75

Comfort Sweet

All God's glory and beauty come from within, and there
He delights to dwell. His visits there are frequent, His
conversation sweet, His comforts refreshing, His peace
passing all understanding.

THOMAS À KEMPIS

❧

God comforts. He doesn't pity.
He picks us up, dries our tears, soothes our fears,
and lifts our thoughts beyond the hurt.

ROBERT SCHULLER

❧

The peace of God, which surpasses all understanding,
will guard your hearts and minds through Christ Jesus.

PHILIPPIANS 4:7 NKJV

❧

God comforts. He lays His right hand
on the wounded soul...and He says, as if that one
were the only soul in all the universe:
O greatly beloved, fear not: peace be unto thee.

AMY CARMICHAEL

There is a place of comfort sweet
Near to the heart of God,
A place where we our Savior meet,
Near to the heart of God....
Hold us who wait before Thee
Near to the heart of God.

CLELAND B. MCAFEE

Every now and again take a good look at something
not made with hands—a mountain, a star,
the turn of a stream. There will come to you wisdom
and patience and solace and, above all,
the assurance that you are not alone in the world.

SIDNEY LOVETT

God is our merciful Father and the source of all comfort.

2 CORINTHIANS 1:3 NLT

God of Promise

For as the rain comes down, and the snow from heaven,
and do not return there, but water the earth,
and make it bring forth and bud, that it may give seed
to the sower and bread to the eater, so shall My word be
that goes forth from My mouth; it shall not return
to Me void, but it shall accomplish what I please,
and it shall prosper in the thing for which I sent it.

ISAIAH 55:10–11 NKJV

God writes with a pen that never blots,
speaks with a tongue that never slips,
and acts with a hand that never fails.

HUBERT VAN ZELLER

The most glorious promises of God are generally fulfilled
in such a wondrous manner that He steps forth to save us
at a time when there is the least appearance of it.

KARL HEINRICH VON BOGATZKY

Be assured, if you walk with Him and look to Him
and expect help from Him, He will never fail you.

GEORGE MUELLER

The light of God surrounds me;
The love of God enfolds me;
The power of God protects me;
The presence of God watches over me.
Wherever I am, God is.

God is the God of promise. He keeps His word,
even when that seems impossible.

COLIN URQUHART

The LORD always keeps his promises;
he is gracious in all he does.

PSALM 145:13 NLT

Absolute Certainty

The hope we have in Christ is an absolute certainty. We can be sure that the place Christ is preparing for us will be ready when we arrive, because with Him nothing is left to chance. Everything He promised He will deliver.

BILLY GRAHAM

❧

Thank the Lord, it is His love that arranges our tomorrows—and we may be certain that whatever tomorrow brings, His love sent it our way.

CHARLES SWINDOLL

❧

Faith is a living, daring confidence in God's grace, so sure and certain that we could stake our life on it a thousand times.

MARTIN LUTHER

❧

Before me, even as behind, God is, and all is well.

JOHN GREENLEAF WHITTIER

There is the firm commitment to the triumph of the human spirit over adversity, the certainty that there's a God on high who may not move mountains but will give you the strength to climb.

GENEVA SMITHERMAN

It is not objective proof of God's existence that we want but the experience of God's presence.
That is the miracle we are really after, and that is also, I think, the miracle that we really get.

FREDERICK BUECHNER

Now faith is confidence in what we hope for and assurance about what we do not see.

HEBREWS 11:1 NIV

Radiant Grace

What do I love when I love You? Not material beauty
or beauty of a temporal order; not the brilliance of earthly
light, so welcome to our eyes; not the sweet melody
of harmony and song.... And yet, when I love Him, it
is true that I love a light of a certain kind that I love in
my inner self, when my soul is bathed in light that is not
bound by space; when it listens to sound that never dies
away; when it breathes fragrance that is not borne away
on the wind.... This is what I love when I love my God.

AUGUSTINE

❧

Joy is not happiness so much as gladness;
it is the ecstasy of eternity in a soul that has
made peace with God and is ready to do His will.

❧

He made you so you could share in His creation,
could love and laugh and know Him.

TED GRIFFEN

Grace creates liberated laughter.
The grace of God...is beautiful, and it radiates joy.

KARL BARTH

❧

Why did God give us imaginations?
Because they help unfold His kingdom.
Imagination unveils the Great Imaginer.
In the beginning, God created.
He imagined the world into being.
Every flower, animal, mountain, and rainbow
is a product of God's creative imagination.

JILL M. RICHARDSON

❧

For the LORD God is our sun and our shield.
He gives us grace and glory.

PSALM 84:11 NLT

God of Grace

Look deep within yourself and recognize what brings life
and grace into your heart. It is this that can be shared
with those around you. You are loved by God.
This is an inspiration to love.

CHRISTOPHER DE VINCK

The value of a person is not measured on an applause
meter; it is measured in the heart and mind of God.
Any believer can rest assured, for on God's scale,
the needle always reads high.

JOHN FISHER

The Lord's chief desire is to reveal Himself to you and,
in order for Him to do that, He gives you abundant
grace. The Lord gives you the experience of enjoying His
presence. He touches you, and His touch is so delightful
that, more than ever, you are drawn inwardly to Him.

MADAME JEANNE GUYON

It is my calling to treat every human being with grace and
dignity, to treat every person, whether encountered in a
palace or a gas station, as a life made in the image of God.

SHEILA WALSH

God be thanked for that good and perfect gift,
the gift unspeakable: His life, His love,
His very self in Christ Jesus.

MALTBIE D. BABCOCK

Set your hope on the grace to be brought to you
when Jesus Christ is revealed.

I PETER I:I3 NIV

Forever Grace

Grace is the dynamic outpouring of God's
loving nature that flows into and through creation
in an endless self-offering of healing, love, illumination,
and reconciliation. It is a gift that we are free to ignore,
reject, ask for, or simply accept.

GERALD G. MAY

❧

Grow in the grace and knowledge of our Lord and Savior
Jesus Christ. To him be glory both now and forever!
Amen.

2 PETER 3:18 NIV

❧

He has caused his wonders to be remembered;
the LORD is gracious and compassionate.... The works
of his hands are faithful and just; all his precepts are
trustworthy. They are established for ever and ever,
enacted in faithfulness and uprightness. He provided
redemption for his people; he ordained his covenant
forever—holy and awesome is his name.

PSALM 111:4, 7–9 NIV

We have been given the breath of life, designed with
a unique, one-of-a-kind soul that exists forever—
whether we live it as a burden or a joy or with indifference
doesn't change the fact that we've been given
the gift of being now and forever.

WENDY MOORE

Let Jesus be in your heart, eternity in your spirit,
the world under your feet, the will of God in your actions.
And let the love of God shine forth from you.

CATHERINE OF GENOA

Just as sin ruled over all people and brought them
to death, now God's wonderful grace rules instead,
giving us right standing with God and resulting
in eternal life through Jesus Christ our Lord.

ROMANS 5:21 NLT

Seeking Hearts

In extravagance of soul we seek His face.
In generosity of heart, we glean His gentle touch.
In excessiveness of spirit, we love Him and His love
comes back to us a hundredfold.

TRICIA MCCARY RHODES

~∾~

I have been away and come back again many times to
this place. Each time I approach, I regret ever having left.
There is a peace here, a serenity, even before I enter. Just
the idea of returning becomes a balm for the wounds I've
collected elsewhere. Before I can finish even one knock,
the door opens wide and I am in His presence.

BARBARA FARMER

~∾~

The simple fact of being...in the presence of the Lord
and of showing Him all that I think, feel, sense,
and experience, without trying to hide anything,
must please Him. Somehow, somewhere,
I know that He loves me.

HENRI J. M. NOUWEN

God's holy beauty comes near you, like a spiritual scent,
and it stirs your drowsing soul.... He creates in you
the desire to find Him and run after Him—to follow
wherever He leads you, and to press peacefully against
His heart wherever He is.

JOHN OF THE CROSS

Once the seeking heart finds God in personal experience
there will be no problem about loving Him.
To know Him is to love Him and to know Him better
is to love Him more.

A. W. TOZER

You will seek me and find me when you seek me
with all your heart.

JEREMIAH 29:13 NIV

Immeasurable Love

We are so preciously loved by God that we cannot even comprehend it. No created being can ever know how much and how sweetly and tenderly God loves them. It is only with the help of His grace that we are able to persevere in spiritual contemplation with endless wonder at His high, surpassing, immeasurable love which our Lord in His goodness has for us.

JULIAN OF NORWICH

God loved us, and through his grace he gave us a good hope and encouragement that continues forever.

2 THESSALONIANS 2:17 NCV

The loving God we serve has immeasurable compassion and tenderness toward each of us throughout our lives.

DR. JAMES DOBSON

The soul is a temple, and God is silently building it
by night and by day. Precious thoughts are building it;
unselfish love is building it;
all-penetrating faith is building it.

HENRY WARD BEECHER

Keep me as the apple of Your eye;
hide me under the shadow of Your wings.

PSALM 17:8 NKJV

Our greatness rests solely on the fact that God in His
incomprehensible goodness has bestowed His love upon
us. God does not love us because we are so valuable;
we are valuable because God loves us.

HELMUT THIELICKE

Seek the Lord

If you are seeking after God, you may be sure of this:
God is seeking you much more. He is the Lover, and you
are His beloved. He has promised Himself to you.

JOHN OF THE CROSS

～⚬～

Ask and it will be given to you; seek and you will find;
knock and the door will be opened to you. For everyone
who asks receives; he who seeks finds; and to him who
knocks, the door will be opened.

MATTHEW 7:7–8 NIV

～⚬～

Prayer enlarges the heart until it is capable
of containing God's gift of Himself. Ask and seek,
and your heart will grow big enough to receive Him
and keep Him as your own.

MOTHER TERESA

～⚬～

To seek God means first of all to let yourself
be found by Him.

God has put into each of our lives a void that cannot
be filled by the world. We may leave God or put Him
on hold, but He is always there,
patiently waiting for us...to turn back to Him.

EMILIE BARNES

❧

Seek the LORD your God, and you will find Him if you
seek Him with all your heart and with all your soul.

DEUTERONOMY 4:29 NKJV

❧

God is not an elusive dream or a phantom to chase,
but a divine person to know. He does not avoid us,
but seeks us. When we seek Him,
the contact is instantaneous.

NEVA COYLE

His Great Love

Most people would not be willing to die for an upright
person, though someone might perhaps be willing to die
for a person who is especially good. But God showed his
great love for us by sending Christ to die for us while we
were still sinners. And since we have been made right in
God's sight by the blood of Christ, he will certainly save
us from God's condemnation. For since our friendship
with God was restored by the death of his Son while
we were still his enemies, we will certainly be saved
through the life of his Son. So now we can rejoice in our
wonderful new relationship with God because our Lord
Jesus Christ has made us friends of God.

ROMANS 5:7–11 NLT

The beauty of grace—our only permanent
deliverance from guilt—is that it meets us where
we are and gives us what we don't deserve.

CHARLES R. SWINDOLL

Be still, and in the quiet moments, listen to the voice
of your heavenly Father. His words can renew your spirit...
no one knows you and your needs like He does.

JANET L. SMITH

∽ஒஒ∾

I will praise you, Lord, among the nations;
I will sing of you among the peoples.
For great is your love, reaching to the heavens;
your faithfulness reaches to the skies.

PSALM 57:9–10 NIV

∽ஒஒ∾

Love is there for us, love so great that it does not turn
its face away from us. That Love is Jesus.
We can dare to hope and believe again.

GLORIA GAITHER

Heart of the Matter

The heart...is the human spirit, and the only thing in us
that God will accept as the basis of our relationship
to Him. It is the spiritual plane of our natural existence,
the place of truth before God, from where alone our
whole lives can become eternal.

DALLAS WILLARD

❧

Search me, God, and know my heart;
test me and know my anxious thoughts.

PSALM 139:23 NIV

❧

We invite the Lord to search our hearts to the depths....
This is a scrutiny of love. We boldly speak the words
of the Psalmist, "Search me, O God, and know my heart;
test me and know my thoughts."

RICHARD J. FOSTER

In the cellar of your heart lurk the ghosts of yesterday's
sins. Sins you've confessed; errors of which you've
repented; damage you've done your best to repair....
Do yourself a favor. Purge your cellar. Exorcise your
basement. Take the Roman nails of Calvary and board up
the door. And remember...He forgot.

MAX LUCADO

❧

He who searches our hearts knows the mind
of the Spirit, because the Spirit intercedes for God's
people in accordance with the will of God.

ROMANS 8:27 NIV

❧

Pour out your heart to God your Father.
He understands you better than you do.

Made Whole

The precious truth of Jesus' power as Redeemer
is that He has a plan and an ability to progressively
restore the broken parts of human experience
and to reproduce a whole person.

JACK HAYFORD

Praise be to the God and Father of our Lord Jesus Christ,
who has blessed us in the heavenly realms with every
spiritual blessing in Christ. For he chose us in him before
the creation of the world to be holy and blameless in his
sight. In love he predestined us for adoption to sonship
through Jesus Christ, in accordance with his pleasure
and will—to the praise of his glorious grace,
which he has freely given us in the One he loves.

EPHESIANS 1:3–6 NIV

The Creator of all thinks enough of you to have sent
Someone very special so that you might have life—
abundantly, joyfully, completely, and victoriously.

God did not tell us to follow Him because
He needed our help, but because He knew that loving
Him would make us whole.

IRENAEUS

❧

Lord, let the glow of Your love
Through my whole being shine;
Fill me with gladness from above
And hold me by strength divine.

MARGARET FISHBACK POWERS

❧

May the God of peace make you holy in every way,
and may your whole spirit and soul and body be kept
blameless until our Lord Jesus Christ comes again.

1 THESSALONIANS 5:23 NLT

He Understands

God possesses infinite knowledge and an awareness which
is uniquely His. At all times, even in the midst of any type
of suffering, I can realize that He knows, loves, watches,
understands, and more than that, He has a purpose.

BILLY GRAHAM

❧

Life from the Center is a life of unhurried peace and
power. It is simple. It is serene.... We need not get frantic.
He is at the helm.

THOMAS R. KELLY

❧

God takes care of His own. He knows our needs.
He anticipates our crises. He is moved by our weaknesses.
He stands ready to come to our rescue. And at just
the right moment He steps in and proves Himself
as our faithful heavenly Father.

CHARLES SWINDOLL

God waits for us in the inner sanctuary of the soul.
He welcomes us there.

RICHARD J. FOSTER

༄

What matters supremely is not the fact that I know
God, but the larger fact which underlies it—the fact that
He knows me. I am graven on the palms of His hands.
I am never out of His mind. All my knowledge of Him
depends on His sustained initiative in knowing me.
I know Him because He first knew me,
and continues to know me.

J. I. PACKER

༄

If anyone loves God, he is known by Him.

1 CORINTHIANS 8:3 NASB

Rich Grace

The LORD gives righteousness and justice to all who are
treated unfairly.... He will not constantly accuse us,
nor remain angry forever. He does not punish us for all
our sins; he does not deal harshly with us,
as we deserve. For his unfailing love toward those
who fear him is as great as the height of the heavens
above the earth. He has removed our sins
as far from us as the east is from the west.

PSALM 103:6, 9–12 NLT

There is an essential connection between experiencing
God, loving God, and trusting God.
You will trust God only as much as you love Him,
and you will love Him to the extent you have touched
Him, rather that He has touched you.

BRENNAN MANNING

Out of his fullness we have all received grace
in place of grace already given.

JOHN 1:16 NIV

God's fingers can touch nothing
but to mold it into loveliness.

GEORGE MACDONALD

✧

Lord...give me only Your love and Your grace.
With this I am rich enough, and I have no more to ask.

IGNATIUS OF LOYOLA

✧

His overflowing love delights to make us partakers
of the bounties He graciously imparts.

HANNAH MORE

✧

LORD, be gracious to us; we long for you.
Be our strength every morning.

ISAIAH 33:2 NIV

He Is More

Although it be good to think upon the kindness of God,
and to love Him and worship Him for it; yet it is far
better to gaze upon the pure essence of Him and to love
Him and worship Him for Himself. We desire many
things, and God offers us only one thing. He *can* offer us
only one thing—Himself. He has nothing else to give.
There *is* nothing else to give.

PETER KREEFT

Who in the skies above can compare with the Lord?
Who is like the Lord among the heavenly beings?
In the council of the holy ones God is greatly feared;
he is more awesome than all who surround him.

PSALM 89:6–7 NIV

In that place of humble thanks, God exalts and gives more
gifts and more of Himself. Which humbles and lays the
soul down lower. And [our] good God responds with
greater gifts of grace and even more of Himself.

ANN VOSKAMP

Wonderful the matchless grace of Jesus,
Deeper than the mighty rolling sea;
Wonderful grace, all sufficient for me, for even me.
Broader than the scope of my transgressions,
Greater far than all my sin and shame,
O magnify the precious Name of Jesus.
Praise His Name!

HALDOR LILLENAS

The LORD is exalted over all the nations,
his glory above the heavens. Who is like the LORD our
God, the One who sits enthroned on high, who stoops
down to look on the heavens and the earth?

PSALM 113:4–6 NIV

You're Invited

Come to me, all you who are weary and burdened,
and I will give you rest. Take my yoke upon you and learn
from me, for I am gentle and humble in heart,
and you will find rest for your souls.
For my yoke is easy and my burden is light.

MATTHEW 11:28–30 NIV

❧

God still draws near to us in the ordinary,
commonplace, everyday experiences and places....
He comes in surprising ways.

HENRY GARIEPY

❧

The LORD longs to be gracious to you; therefore he will
rise up to show you compassion.

ISAIAH 30:18 NIV

It's like an invitation to visit with God, to watch the clouds break up and disappear, leaving behind a blue patch of sky and bright sunshine that is so warm upon my face. It's a glimpse of divinity; a kiss from heaven.

God is here! I hear His voice
While thrushes make the woods rejoice.
I touch His robe each time I place
My hand against a pansy's face.
I breathe His breath if I but pass
Verbenas trailing through the grass.
God is here! From every tree
His leafy fingers beckon me.

MADELEINE AARON

You've always given me breathing room, a place
to get away from it all, a lifetime pass to your safe-house,
an open invitation as your guest.

PSALM 61:3 MSG

Encountering God

We encounter God in the ordinariness of life,
not in the search for spiritual highs and extraordinary,
mystical experiences, but in our simple presence in life.

BRENNAN MANNING

❦

God is with us in the midst of our daily,
routine lives. In the middle of cleaning the house
or driving somewhere in the pickup....
Often it's in the middle of the most mundane
task that He lets us know He is there with us.
We realize, then, that there can be no "ordinary"
moments for people who live their lives with Jesus.

MICHAEL CARD

❦

This is how we know that he lives in us:
We know it by the Spirit he gave us.

1 JOHN 3:24 NIV

Do you believe that God is near? He wants you to.
He wants you to know that He is in the midst of your
world. Wherever you are as you read these words,
He is present. In your car. On the plane. In your office,
your bedroom, your den. He's near.
And He is more than near. He is active.

MAX LUCADO

❧

Much of what is sacred is hidden in the ordinary,
everyday moments of our lives. To see something
of the sacred in those moments takes slowing down so we
can live our lives more reflectively.

KEN GIRE

❧

If each moment is sacred—a time and place
where we encounter God—life itself is sacred.

JEAN M. BLOMQUIST

Full Restoration

Whatever your loss, pain, failure, or brokenness,
Jesus Christ is fully capable of bringing about change unto
full restoration. Just as His resurrection power brings new
life, His redemption power brings new hope. He is able,
for He's more than a Savior! He's your Redeemer who
promises that He will give "beauty for ashes,
the oil of joy for mourning" (Isaiah 61:3 KJV).

JACK HAYFORD

Jesus Himself conquered death, hell, and the grave.
Nothing could hold Him down. He rose from the grave
on that third victorious day. And now that same power
that raised Jesus from the dead lives in us! We don't have
to be chained to sin and death any longer.

MICHAEL NEALE

Create in me a pure heart, O God, and renew a steadfast
spirit within me. Do not cast me from your presence or
take your Holy Spirit from me. Restore to me the joy of
your salvation and grant me a willing spirit, to sustain me.

PSALM 51:10−12 NIV

Cast your burden on the Lord, and He shall sustain you.

PSALM 55:22 NKJV

It is through our encounter with God
that we reaches our highest destiny.

CAROL GISH

I love those who love me;
and those who diligently seek me will find me.

PROVERBS 8:17 NASB

New Life

Since we believe that Christ died for all, we also believe
that we have all died to our old life. He died for everyone
so that those who receive his new life will no longer live
for themselves. Instead, they will live for Christ, who died
and was raised for them. So we have stopped evaluating
others from a human point of view. At one time
we thought of Christ merely from a human point of view.
How differently we know him now! This means that
anyone who belongs to Christ has become a new person.
The old life is gone; a new life has begun!
And all of this is a gift from God.

2 CORINTHIANS 5:14–18 NLT

Once more to new creation
Awake, and death gainsay,
For death is swallowed up of life,
And Christ is risen today!

GEORGE NEWELL LOVEJOY

The resurrection gives my life meaning
and direction and the opportunity to start over
no matter what my circumstances.

ROBERT FLATT

⌘

Every day we live is a priceless gift of God,
loaded with possibilities to learn something new,
to gain fresh insights.

DALE EVANS ROGERS

⌘

Let the Spirit renew your thoughts and attitudes.
Put on your new nature, created to be like God—
truly righteous and holy.

EPHESIANS 4:23–24 NLT

Our Destiny

This is our destiny in heaven—to be like Christ:
not Christ limited, as He was on earth, to the confines
of time and flesh, but Christ risen, the great,
free, timeless Christ of the Easter morning.

DAVID WINTER

~❧~

Our confidence in the future is based firmly
on the fact of what God has done for us in Christ.
No matter what our situation may be, we need never
despair because Christ is alive.

BILLY GRAHAM

~❧~

Recognizing who we are in Christ and aligning our life
with God's purpose for us gives a sense of destiny....
It gives form and direction to our life.

JEAN FLEMING

I feel simply carried along each hour, doing my part
in a plan which is far beyond myself. This sense
of cooperation with God in little things is what so
astonishes me, for I never have felt this way before.
I need something, and turn round to find it
waiting for me. I must work, to be sure,
but there is God working along with me.

I still belong to you; you hold my right hand.
You guide me with your counsel, leading me
to a glorious destiny. Whom have I in heaven but you?
I desire you more than anything on earth.
My health may fail, and my spirit may grow weak,
but God remains the strength of my heart;
he is mine forever.

PSALM 73:23–26 NLT

He Walks with Us

In the ultimate alchemy of all history, God took the worst thing that could possibly happen—the appalling execution of the innocent Son—and turned it into the final victory over evil and death. It was an act of unprecedented cunning, turning the design of evil into the service of good, an act that holds within it a promise for all of us.

PHILIP YANCEY

∽⧬∾

I will walk among you; I will be your God,
and you will be my people.

LEVITICUS 26:12 NLT

∽⧬∾

The Lord our shepherd is with us, in the valley or even in the face of death, sharing a meal of friendship, giving us all that we need and more.

MICHAEL NEALE

The LORD is my shepherd;
I shall not want.
He makes me to lie down in green pastures;
He leads me beside the still waters.
He restores my soul;
He leads me in the paths of righteousness
For His name's sake.
Yea, though I walk through the valley
of the shadow of death, I will fear no evil;
For You are with me;
Your rod and Your staff, they comfort me.
You prepare a table before me
in the presence of my enemies;
You anoint my head with oil;
My cup runs over.
Surely goodness and mercy shall follow me
All the days of my life;
And I will dwell in the house of the LORD
Forever.

PSALM 23 NKJV

He Pays Attention

God gets down on His knees among us; gets on our level
and shares Himself with us. He does not reside afar off
and send diplomatic messages, He kneels among us....
God shares Himself generously and graciously.

EUGENE PETERSON

If you believe in God, it is not too difficult to believe that
He is concerned about the universe and all the events on
this earth. But the really staggering message of the Bible
is that this same God cares deeply about you and your
identity and the events of your life.

BRUCE LARSON

I don't mean to say that I have already achieved
these things or that I have already reached perfection.
But I press on to possess that perfection for which
Christ Jesus first possessed me.

PHILIPPIANS 3:12 NLT

The God who created, names, and numbers the stars in the heavens also numbers the hairs of my head.... He pays attention to very big things and to very small ones. What matters to me matters to Him, and that changes my life.

ELISABETH ELLIOT

I am with you and will watch over you wherever you go.

GENESIS 28:15 NIV

A new path lies before us;
We're not sure where it leads;
But God goes on before us,
Providing all our needs.
This path, so new, so different
Exciting as we climb,
Will guide us in His perfect will
Until the end of time.

LINDA MAURICE

A Message for Us

What we need to know, of course, is not just that God
exists, not just that beyond the steely brightness
of the stars there is a cosmic intelligence...but that there
is a God right here in the thick of our day-by-day lives
who may not be writing messages about Himself
in the stars but in one way or another is trying to get
messages through our blindness.

FREDERICK BUECHNER

The Empty Tomb had a message for the disciples
as it has for us.
It says to science and philosophy, "Explain this event."
It says to history, "Repeat this event."
It says to time, "Blot out this event."
It says to faith, "Believe this event.

PAUL LEE TAN

This resurrection life you received from God is not
a timid, grave-tending life. It's adventurously expectant,
greeting God with a childlike "What's next, Papa?" God's
Spirit touches our spirits and confirms who we really are.
We know who he is, and we know who we are: Father and
children. And we know we are going to get what's coming
to us—an unbelievable inheritance!

ROMANS 8:15–16 MSG

Wherever we look in the realm of nature,
we see evidence for God's design and exquisite care for
His creatures. Whether we examine the cosmos on its
largest scale or its tiniest, His handiwork is evident....
God's fingerprints are visible.

DR. HUGH ROSS

Love. No greater theme can be emphasized.
No stronger message can be proclaimed.

CHARLES SWINDOLL

Changed by Grace

Your grace, how it's sufficient for me, how it carries all my
burdens and displaces my iniquity. When the Father gazes
down no longer does he see the reflection of a wicked
man, but the man who died on Calvary.

REILLY

∽⤫⤳

Do not pray for easy lives. Pray to be stronger.
Do not pray for tasks equal to your powers. Pray for
powers equal to your tasks. Then the doing of your work
shall be no miracle, but you shall be the miracle.

PHILLIPS BROOKS

∽⤫⤳

It was not with perishable things such as silver or gold
that you were redeemed from the empty way of life...but
with the precious blood of Christ.

1 PETER 1:18–19 NIV